Healing From Childhood Trauma and Hidden Abuse

A Survival Guide to Recovery From Childhood Trauma and Psychological Abuse
Klish T. Kinderman

Copyright ©

Klish T. Kinderman
© 2023 United Kingdom

All rights reserved. No part of this book may be reproduced or modified in any form, including photocopying, recording, or by any information storage and retrieval system, without permission in writing from the publisher.

Table of Contents

Title Page 1
Copyright Page 2
Introduction 4
Chapter One | Effects of Childhood Trauma 6
Chapter Two | Stages of Healing From Childhood Trauma 11
Chapter Three | Effective Ways to Heal from Childhood Trauma ... 16
Chapter Four | Available Treatment to Help Recover from Childhood Trauma 23
Chapter Five | How to Recover from Rape and Sexual Trauma 28
Chapter Six | How to Build Your Self-Esteem After Experiencing Abuse 36
Conclusion 43

Introduction

Childhood trauma refers to experiences that children have during their early years that are deeply distressing, overwhelming, and harmful to their physical, emotional, and psychological well-being.

Childhood trauma can take many forms, including physical, sexual, or emotional abuse, neglect, witnessing domestic violence, separation from a primary caregiver, natural disasters, or other traumatic events.

These experiences can have a profound and lasting impact on a child's development, affecting their ability to form healthy relationships, regulate their emotions, and cope with stress.

Childhood trauma can also lead to a range of mental health issues, including depression, anxiety, post-traumatic stress disorder (PTSD), and other psychological disorders.

It's vital to note that not all children who experience trauma will develop long-term negative effects, and the severity of the trauma and the child's individual resilience can play a role in determining the outcome.

However, early identification and treatment of childhood trauma can greatly improve a child's chances of recovery and prevent future difficulties.

Childhood trauma and hidden abuse can have a lasting effect on an individual's emotional and mental well-being.

As adults, it can be hard to recover from experiences that we may not even remember or be aware of.

Many survivors of childhood trauma feel like they are alone in their experience and struggle to find the resources they need to heal.

However, there is hope for those who are looking to address their trauma as adults in order to lead healthier lives.

Recovering from childhood trauma as an adult is possible, but it requires dedication and commitment to the healing process.

Fortunately, there are steps that adults can take to begin the healing process and regain control of their lives.

This book explores different methods of healing from childhood trauma as an adult, providing effective strategies and resources to those looking to take back their power and begin their healing journey.

Without much ado, let's get right into it.

Chapter One
Effects of Childhood Trauma

Childhood trauma can have profound and lasting effects on an individual's mental and physical health.

Traumatic experiences such as sexual abuse, emotional abuse, neglect, or exposure to violence can cause a range of emotional problems, such as anxiety, depression, mood disorders, and substance abuse.

Below are examples of common effects experienced by people who are going through childhood trauma.

Academic underachievement

Childhood trauma can have a profound impact on academic achievement in adulthood. Trauma, such as physical abuse, neglect, or psychological abuse during childhood, can lead to anxiety and depression later in life. These mental health issues often result in difficulty concentrating and retaining information necessary for academic success.

Moreover, the effects of childhood trauma may also manifest as behavioral problems that affect academic performance.

For instance, individuals who experienced abuse or neglect may develop coping mechanisms such as dissociation or avoidance that can hinder their ability to engage with schoolwork.

Additionally, some individuals who experience childhood trauma may struggle with relationships and forming social connections with peers and authority figures like teachers.

In conclusion, it is essential to recognize the long-term effects of childhood trauma on academic outcomes. Providing support systems that address both mental health concerns and behavioral issues can help adult survivors of childhood trauma overcome the challenges they face in achieving academic success.

Under-responding or over-responding to emotional events

Childhood trauma can have a terrible impact on how adults respond to emotional events. Those who have experienced trauma in their childhood may develop an under-response or over-response to emotional events, which could be harmful to their mental health and relationships.

For instance, individuals who have experienced neglect or abuse as children may find it challenging to recognize and express emotions appropriately.

Under-responding to emotional events is a common response among adults who have undergone childhood trauma. They may find it hard to understand and regulate their emotions, leading them not to feel anything at all. This lack of emotion can cause problems with personal relationships and career success since they don't know how to react appropriately in various situations.

On the other hand, over-responding is another typical response that survivors of childhood trauma experience.

They often become easily overwhelmed by their emotions, such as anger or anxiety, even if the situation doesn't warrant it.

This kind of reaction can lead them towards more stress and affect their abilities for decision-making while increasing the chances of developing mood disorders like depression and anxiety.

Changes in behavior or communication

Childhood trauma can have a profound impact on an individual's behavior and communication style into adulthood. The traumatic experiences that one faced in their early years can alter the way one interacts with others, leading to changes such as social withdrawal, aggression, or anxiety. Adults who experienced childhood trauma may struggle with attachment issues or have difficulty forming close relationships due to trust issues.

Moreover, childhood trauma can result in altered communication patterns. For instance, survivors of abuse may become withdrawn or avoidant while communicating with others about their feelings or thoughts.

On the other hand, some individuals who faced childhood adversity may become overly aggressive when communicating due to being defensive and fearful of being hurt again.

In conclusion, understanding how childhood trauma can impact behavior and communication is crucial for developing effective strategies for healing and recovery.

Through counseling or therapy sessions focused on addressing these concerns and learning coping mechanisms, adults can start to overcome the challenges created by previous traumatic experiences.

A heightened sense of hyper-vigilance

Childhood trauma can result in a heightened sense of hypervigilance, anxiousness, clinginess, chronic worry, or explosive anger in adults.

These symptoms often stem from the traumatic experiences that individuals endured during their childhood years.

As children who have experienced trauma grow older, they may develop maladaptive coping mechanisms to deal with their intense emotions.

For instance, hypervigilance and anxiety are common symptoms of post-traumatic stress disorder (PTSD).

Children who experience traumatic events such as abuse or neglect may become hyperaware of their surroundings and always be on guard for potential threats. This can lead to heightened anxiety and difficulty relaxing even in safe environments. Similarly, clinginess and chronic worry can be signs that an individual is struggling to cope with unresolved trauma from childhood.

Finally, explosive anger is another symptom that adults who experienced childhood trauma may exhibit.

This type of anger is often triggered by situations that remind them of past traumas which could not have been handled when young due to a lack of emotional maturity or resources.

It's important for individuals experiencing these symptoms to seek professional help from a mental health provider specializing in treating PTSD and other childhood-related traumas so they can learn healthy coping mechanisms and strategies to manage their emotions effectively.

Dysregulation related to depression and despondency

Childhood trauma is a significant risk factor for the development of mental health issues, including depression and anxiety.

When children experience trauma, their emotional and physical responses can become dysregulated, leading to long-term difficulties in managing emotions and behaviors.

As adults, these individuals may struggle with depression or despondency due to an inability to regulate their emotional responses effectively.

Additionally, childhood trauma can lead to a lack of motivation or lethargy, as individuals may feel overwhelmed by their traumatic experiences.

They may also struggle with focusing on tasks or activities as they are easily distracted by intrusive thoughts related to their trauma. This difficulty with attention and focus can impact various areas of life, such as work or relationships.

Finally, childhood trauma can result in social withdrawal or isolation, as individuals may struggle with trust issues and feel uncomfortable forming close relationships.

The resulting quietness from this isolation can be mistaken for shyness when it's more likely that the individual struggles with feelings of safety and self-worth.

Overall, it's essential that individuals who have experienced childhood trauma seek professional help to learn skills for regulating emotions effectively so that they may lead healthy, fulfilling lives.

Chronic illness

Childhood trauma can have long-lasting effects on the physical health of adults. Research has shown that individuals who experienced adverse childhood experiences (ACEs) are at a higher risk for developing chronic illnesses and diseases later in life.

One way this can manifest is through irritable bowel syndrome (IBS), which is characterized by abdominal pain, bloating, constipation, or diarrhea.

The exact cause of IBS is still unknown, but studies suggest that childhood trauma can lead to alterations in the gut microbiome and increased inflammation, both of which may contribute to IBS symptoms.

In addition to IBS, chronic fatigue syndrome (CFS) is another illness that may result from childhood trauma.

CFS is a debilitating condition that causes extreme fatigue and weakness that cannot be explained by an underlying medical condition. Studies have it that individuals with a history of ACEs are more likely to develop CFS later in life than those without such experiences. It's believed that the chronic stress caused by childhood trauma can lead to dysregulation of the immune system and increased inflammation, both of which may play a role in CFS development.

Lastly, individuals who experienced childhood trauma may also be prone to injury or illness due to their altered stress response system.

Trauma can cause prolonged activation of the body's fight-or-flight response, leading to chronically elevated levels of cortisol (the stress hormone).

This heightened state of stress can weaken the immune system over time and result in increased susceptibility to injuries and illnesses.

Having looked at some of the major signs and symptoms associated with childhood trauma, let's now look at strategies that can help you recover from this mental health condition.

But first, we will be looking at the three major stages of childhood trauma recovery.

See you in the next chapter...

Chapter Two
Stages of Healing From Childhood Trauma

Everyone's experience with healing from childhood trauma is unique; therefore, there isn't a predetermined or prescribed way to do it.

This can vary according to whether or not you are still in contact with childhood offenders, your family's structure, which affects whether or not certain incidents can be discussed, or current events and circumstances in your life.

However, the majority of those who have gone through this share certain experiences and steps for healing childhood trauma.

When recovering from childhood trauma, you could go through the following three stages:

Getting real

When it comes to healing from childhood trauma, getting real is one of the most important stages.

This stage involves acknowledging and accepting the fact that you were indeed traumatized as a child and that this trauma has had lasting effects on your life. It means facing the difficult emotions and memories associated with your past experiences.

Getting real also involves being honest with yourself about how these experiences have influenced your thoughts, feelings, and behaviors in the present.

This requires a great deal of self-reflection and introspection. It may involve seeking therapy or other forms of professional support to help you process your emotions and come to terms with your past.

Ultimately, getting real is an essential step toward healing from childhood trauma.

By acknowledging what happened to you and facing it head-on, you can begin to move forward with greater clarity and purpose in your life. While it may be a difficult process at times, it is ultimately worth the effort for those who are committed to their own growth and well-being.

Acceptance

Acceptance is a crucial stage in the healing process from childhood trauma. It involves acknowledging and coming to terms with the reality of what happened without minimizing or denying the impact it had on one's life.

Acceptance is not about condoning abuse or excusing the actions of those who caused the trauma but rather allowing oneself to feel and express emotions related to the experience.

During this stage, individuals may experience intense feelings of grief, anger, guilt, and shame as they confront painful memories and emotions that were previously avoided.

While acceptance can be difficult and uncomfortable, it is an essential step towards reclaiming one's power and moving forward in life.

Accepting what has happened also allows individuals to let go of unrealistic expectations for themselves and others that may have been holding them back.

In conclusion, acceptance is a critical component of healing from childhood trauma.

It requires courage, vulnerability, and a willingness to face painful emotions head-on, but ultimately sets the foundation for growth and freedom from past suffering.

Growth Focus

GROWTH FOCUS IS ONE of the stages of healing from childhood trauma. It involves shifting the focus from the past to the present and future.

This stage is characterized by a desire to learn, grow, and develop oneself. Growth focus helps in breaking free from old patterns and habits that may have been developed as a result of childhood trauma.

During this stage, individuals start to set goals for themselves and work towards achieving them.

They begin to identify their strengths and weaknesses while also identifying areas they would like to improve on.

This enables them to develop new skills and talents, which further helps build their confidence.

In conclusion, growth focus plays a crucial role in healing from childhood trauma. It promotes personal development and self-awareness, helping individuals move away from negative experiences that may have affected their lives negatively in the past.

Through growth focus, individuals can take control of their lives again by setting goals that align with their values and working towards achieving them.

The following constructive life improvements can come about as a result of healing from your childhood trauma:

Healed relationships or new relationships that are life-giving

Healing from childhood trauma can have a significant impact on one's ability to form and maintain healthy relationships.

When individuals address the root causes of their trauma, they gain a deeper understanding of themselves and the impact that their experiences have had on their behaviors and beliefs. This self-awareness can lead to more intentional communication and behavior in relationships, resulting in healthier dynamics.

Healed relationships may also result from the process of working through childhood trauma. As individuals learn to heal and grow together, they are able to develop deeper levels of trust, intimacy, and vulnerability.

This allows for greater emotional connection and a stronger bond between partners or loved ones.

In addition, healing from childhood trauma can create space for new life-giving relationships to form.

As individuals become more grounded in their sense of self-worth and value, they are better equipped to attract healthy people into their lives who share similar values and goals.

These relationships can provide support, encouragement, and mutual growth opportunities that contribute positively to overall well-being.

New or renewed choices that result in a significantly better life or future

Healing from childhood trauma can lead to new or renewed choices that result in a significantly better life or future.

One way healing from trauma can lead to positive change is through the development of emotional regulation skills.

Trauma survivors often struggle with regulating their emotions due to the dysregulation caused by traumatic experiences.

Through therapy and other forms of healing, individuals can learn how to regulate their emotions effectively, which can improve their relationships, work performance, and overall quality of life.

Another way healing from childhood trauma can lead to positive change is by increasing self-awareness. Traumatic experiences can cause individuals to dissociate or disconnect from themselves as a means of coping with the pain.

However, this disconnection often leads to difficulties in understanding one's own needs and desires.

Healing from trauma involves reconnecting with oneself and developing a deeper understanding of one's values and goals.

This newfound self-awareness allows individuals to make more intentional choices that align with their values and bring them closer to achieving their goals.

Overall, healing from childhood trauma is a challenging but worthwhile process that has the potential for significant positive change in one's life.

By developing emotional regulation skills and increasing self-awareness, survivors are better equipped to make choices that lead them towards a more fulfilling future.

Improved self-esteem and understanding of the value you bring to your workplace or personal life

Childhood trauma can leave deep emotional scars that can affect one's self-worth, leading to low confidence levels and a negative perception of themselves.

However, by working through the trauma and healing from it, individuals can begin to realize their worth and potential.

Improved self-esteem is often a natural byproduct of healing from childhood trauma. When individuals confront past traumas, they begin to make sense of them and understand how they have shaped who they are today.

This newfound understanding allows them to take control of their emotions, thoughts, and behaviors in ways that promote healthy relationships with themselves and others.

With an improved sense of self-worth comes a greater appreciation for the value one brings to their workplace or personal life.

Individuals who have healed from childhood trauma tend to have more resilience in the face of adversity, possess better-coping mechanisms when handling stressors at work or home, and be more adaptable in new situations.

Overall, healing from childhood trauma has many benefits that extend beyond just overcoming past experiences but also lead to positive changes in various aspects of one's life.

New or renewed life goals and interests

When individuals heal from childhood trauma, they often experience a shift in their priorities and perspectives. This can lead to the development of new or renewed life goals and interests. For example, someone who has experienced neglect as a child may develop a strong desire to form close relationships with loved ones as an adult.

Additionally, healing from trauma can help individuals rediscover their passions and hobbies that were once overshadowed by their traumatic experiences.

They may find themselves drawn towards activities that promote self-care and personal growth, such as meditation or creative expression.

Ultimately, the process of healing from childhood trauma is unique to each individual. However, it can provide a powerful opportunity for personal transformation and the pursuit of fulfilling life goals and interests.

Chapter Three
Effective Ways to Heal from Childhood Trauma

Although children are frequently thought of as being extremely resilient and capable of recovering from almost any scenario, traumatic experiences throughout childhood can have serious and long-lasting impacts that endure far into adulthood if they are not addressed.

Childhood trauma can be caused by anything that leaves a child feeling powerless and alters their perception of safety and security, such as sexual, physical, or verbal abuse; domestic violence; an unstable or unsafe environment; parental separation; neglect; bullying; life-threatening illness; or intrusive medical procedures.

There is hope if you are struggling with the emotional and psychological effects of a difficult childhood. Here are some effective techniques for overcoming childhood trauma and taking back control of your life.

Acknowledge the problem

Acknowledging the problem and its triggers is a crucial first step in healing from childhood trauma. When an adult recognizes that they have experienced trauma, it can help them to better understand why they may be struggling with certain emotions or behaviors.

By acknowledging the problem, an adult can begin to take ownership of their experiences and work towards finding ways to heal. Additionally, identifying specific triggers that may cause them to feel anxious or upset can help them avoid situations that may exacerbate their trauma.

Acknowledging the problem and its triggers can also allow for more effective communication with loved ones or mental health professionals. It creates a shared language for discussing past experiences and current struggles, which can lead to greater understanding and support in the healing process. Ultimately, by recognizing the impact of childhood trauma on their lives, adults are empowered to take steps towards recovery and a brighter future.

Love the child inside you

Loving the child inside you can be a powerful tool for adults who have experienced childhood trauma. When we experience traumatic events as children, parts of ourselves become stuck in that time period.

These parts of us continue to carry the pain and fear that we experienced during those moments. By loving and nurturing these inner child parts, we can begin to heal those wounds.

One way to love your inner child is by practicing self-compassion. This means treating yourself with kindness and understanding, no matter what mistakes you may make or how you may feel about yourself. It also involves acknowledging the pain and suffering that your inner child has endured and offering comfort and support.

Another way to connect with your inner child is through playfulness and creativity. Engaging in activities that bring joy or spark your imagination can help unlock feelings of curiosity, wonder, and pleasure.

This not only helps to build a positive relationship with your inner child but also promotes overall well-being by reducing stress levels and enhancing mood.

Use positive affirmations

It is vital to understand that childhood traumas can have a lasting impact on one's mental health, and using positive affirmations is one way to counteract the negative effects of such experiences.

Positive affirmations are statements that are repeated consistently and help to promote self-love, self-acceptance, and self-confidence.

When an individual repeats positive affirmations, they reprogram their thought patterns by replacing negative thoughts with positive ones.

This process helps to boost the individual's sense of self-worth and creates a more optimistic outlook on life. Furthermore, it encourages them to let go of past hurts and allows them to move forward in a healthier way.

Positive affirmations also have physiological effects on the body. They help reduce cortisol levels (the stress hormone) within the body, which can cause physical symptoms such as headaches or stomach problems.

By reducing these symptoms and promoting relaxation within the body, individuals are better able to cope with their past traumas while focusing on creating a brighter future for themselves.

Some examples of positive affirmations include: "I am worthy of love and respect," "I am capable of achieving my goals," "I forgive myself for past mistakes," "I trust my intuition and inner wisdom," and "I release all negative emotions from my past." These affirmations can be adapted to suit your specific situation or needs.

It's important to remember that healing from childhood trauma is a journey, and positive affirmations are just one aspect of the process.

Put an end to negative chatters

Negative self-talk, also known as negative chatters, often stems from childhood trauma. It can manifest as an inner critic that constantly berates oneself with belittling and unhelpful thoughts.

Healing from childhood trauma requires confronting these negative chatters head-on to cultivate a more positive inner dialogue.

One way to put an end to negative chatters is through mindfulness practices like meditation or yoga. These techniques help individuals become aware of their internal dialogue and learn how to replace negative thoughts with more compassionate ones. Another approach is cognitive behavioral therapy (CBT), which helps individuals identify and challenge harmful thought patterns.

It's also important for adults healing from childhood trauma to seek support from trusted friends, family members, or mental health professionals.

Sharing one's experiences in a safe and supportive environment can help reduce shame and isolation while facilitating the healing process.

Overall, ending negative self-talk may be challenging but ultimately worth it in promoting long-term well-being and post-traumatic growth.

Don't blame yourself

BLAMING ONESELF FOR childhood trauma can be a common response, especially when the trauma is caused by someone close to us, such as a parent or caregiver.

However, it's important to understand that no child deserves to experience abuse or neglect, and it's not their fault when they do. It's essential to recognize that the responsibility for the trauma lies solely with the perpetrator and not with the victim.

Accepting this truth can be a significant step in healing from childhood trauma. It allows individuals to let go of any feelings of guilt or shame they may have carried with them for years and shift their focus towards processing their emotions in a healthier way.

Individuals who are going through childhood trauma should treat themselves kindly and acknowledge that what happened was not their fault while working on rebuilding their sense of self-worth and confidence. With time and effort, anyone who has experienced childhood trauma can learn how to heal without putting the blame on themselves, leading to a life full of happiness and fulfillment.

Don't isolate yourself

While it may seem easier to isolate oneself and avoid triggers that could trigger flashbacks or painful memories, this approach can be counterproductive in the long run.

Isolation can lead to social withdrawal, loneliness and worsen the symptoms of trauma.

One effective way for adults to heal from childhood trauma is by seeking support from family members, friends or a licensed therapist.

Sharing one's experiences with someone who understands and empathizes can provide comfort and validation that is essential for healing. Talking about past traumas with trusted individuals also helps release bottled-up emotions such as anger, guilt or shame that might have been repressed over time.

In addition to seeking support from others, self-care practices are vital in healing from childhood trauma.

Getting involved in activities that bring joy, such as exercise, meditation, art therapy or joining support groups, can help reduce stress levels and promote emotional regulation.

When an adult who has suffered childhood trauma takes care of their physical and emotional needs while surrounded by people they trust, they will be able to move beyond the traumatic experience towards healing and recovery.

Let go of past events that you cannot change

While it can be challenging to relinquish control over something that has happened, it is essential to understand that dwelling on the past only keeps you stuck in a negative cycle. It would be of great help to you if you learned how to accept what has happened and move forward with your life.

One technique for letting go of past events is through mindfulness practices such as meditation or yoga.

These practices allow individuals to focus on the present moment rather than dwelling on the past or worrying about the future. Over time, this can help reduce feelings of anxiety and depression caused by childhood trauma.

Don't be hard on yourself

Healing from childhood trauma can be a long and difficult process for adults. However, it is important not to be too hard on yourself during this time.

Healing takes time and patience, and it is important to recognize that progress may come in small steps rather than giant leaps. It is crucial to remember that healing from trauma does not mean erasing the past or forgetting what has happened; instead, it means learning how to cope with these experiences in a healthy way.

Furthermore, giving up on oneself can hinder the healing process. It is common for individuals who have experienced trauma to feel hopeless or believe they will never fully heal.

This negative self-talk can result in feelings of defeat and discourage individuals from seeking help or continuing with their treatment plan.

However, it is important to remember that healing is possible, and there are resources available for those who need them.

In conclusion, while healing from childhood trauma can be challenging, it is essential not to be too hard on oneself or give up hope for a better future.

By taking small steps towards recovery and seeking support when needed, individuals can learn how to cope with their experiences in a healthy way and move forward towards a brighter tomorrow.

Be patient with yourself

Healing from childhood trauma as an adult is not a linear process. It requires patience and compassion towards oneself. When we experience trauma during our developmental years, it can shape our beliefs and behaviors that we carry into adulthood.

Therefore, the healing process may involve unlearning these beliefs and replacing them with healthier ones.

Patience in this journey involves taking small steps towards healing rather than expecting a quick fix. It also means learning to accept setbacks as part of the process without feeling discouraged or defeated.

One way to be patient with ourselves is by practicing self-care regularly, such as engaging in mindfulness practices, seeking therapy or support groups, journaling, or participating in activities that bring us joy.

Finally, being patient with ourselves also means acknowledging that everyone's healing journey is different and unique. We should avoid comparing ourselves to others or setting unrealistic expectations for our progress.

Instead, focus on your growth at your own pace while celebrating each milestone along the way. Ultimately, patience helps us cultivate self-compassion and create space for genuine healing to take place from childhood trauma as an adult.

Recognize and appreciate your progress

Recognizing and appreciating your progress is a crucial step in healing from childhood trauma. As an adult, you may have spent years struggling with the effects of traumatic experiences that occurred in your childhood. However, by acknowledging how far you've come, you can begin to reframe your narrative and see yourself as a survivor instead of a victim.

A good way to do this is by keeping a progress journal where you write down small victories and positive changes you've noticed in your life.

Celebrate each milestone no matter how small it may seem. This will help you build momentum and motivate yourself to keep going.

Ultimately, recognizing and appreciating your progress is about giving yourself permission to celebrate successes while also acknowledging that healing from childhood trauma takes time – but it's possible! With patience, resilience, and self-compassion, anyone can overcome their past experiences to live a fulfilling life.

Seek the help of a professional

Seeking the help of a professional is an effective way for adults to heal from childhood trauma. A qualified therapist can assist clients in identifying and processing past experiences that may be impacting their current mental health. Through various therapeutic techniques, a licensed therapist can guide individuals toward recovery.

One major benefit of seeking professional help is access to a safe and non-judgmental space. Adults who have gone through childhood trauma may struggle with opening up about their past experiences due to fear of stigma or shame.

However, with the support of a trusted therapist, individuals can feel comfortable exploring their emotions and working through any negative thought patterns that may be hindering their progress.

Another advantage of seeking professional help is the development of coping strategies tailored to each individual's specific needs. Trauma affects everyone differently, so it's important for therapists to create personalized treatment plans based on each client's unique experiences and symptoms. These coping mechanisms can include mindfulness exercises, grounding techniques, or self-care practices that are designed to promote long-term healing and overall well-being.

Chapter Four
Available Treatment to Help Recover from Childhood Trauma

Negative repercussions from childhood trauma can manifest now and in the future. The good news is that treatment can assist you in identifying triggers, creating coping mechanisms, and reducing symptoms—all in a secure and encouraging setting.

Here are a few typical therapy approaches for teenagers, adults, and adolescents.

Cognitive processing therapy (CPT)

Cognitive-behavioral therapy (CBT) is an effective treatment for individuals struggling with childhood trauma. This type of therapy is aimed at identifying negative thought patterns and behaviors and replacing them with positive ones.

CBT helps people to change their thinking patterns, which in turn changes their behavior. This can lead to significant improvements in mental health.

CBT sessions typically involve the therapist helping the individual identify specific thoughts or memories that are causing distress.

The therapist will then work with the individual to challenge these negative thoughts and replace them with more positive ones. Over time, this process can help an adult who has experienced childhood trauma to heal from their past experiences.

Overall, cognitive-behavioral therapy is a highly effective way for adults suffering from childhood trauma to overcome their struggles and achieve a greater sense of well-being.

It may take time and effort on the part of both the individual and the therapist, but CBT has been shown to be a successful method for healing from traumatic experiences.

Trauma-focused cognitive behavioral therapy (TF-CBT)

Cognitive-behavioral therapy (CBT) is an effective treatment for individuals struggling with childhood trauma.

This type of therapy is aimed at identifying negative thought patterns and behaviors and replacing them with positive ones. CBT helps people to change their thinking patterns, which in turn changes their behavior. This can lead to significant improvements in mental health.

CBT sessions typically involve the therapist helping the individual identify specific thoughts or memories that are causing distress.

The therapist will then work with the individual to challenge these negative thoughts and replace them with more positive ones. Over time, this process can help an adult who has experienced childhood trauma to heal from their past experiences.

Overall, cognitive-behavioral therapy is a highly effective way for adults suffering from childhood trauma to overcome their struggles and achieve a greater sense of well-being.

It may take time and effort on the part of both the individual and the therapist, but CBT has been shown to be a successful method for healing from traumatic experiences.

Eye movement desensitization and reprocessing (EMDR)

EMDR is a psychotherapy treatment that helps individuals alleviate the distress associated with traumatic memories.

It is based on the idea that trauma symptoms are created by unprocessed memories in the brain.

EMDR uses a structured protocol to help trauma patients activate their natural healing processes, including rapid eye movements while recalling traumatic experiences.

EMDR has been shown to be an effective treatment for various types of trauma, including childhood abuse and neglect.

The process involves identifying specific traumatic memories and using bilateral stimulation techniques such as eye movements or tapping to desensitize the patient's emotional response to those memories.

Through repeated sessions, clients can reprocess their traumas and create new adaptive beliefs about themselves and their world.

While EMDR may not completely eliminate all symptoms associated with childhood trauma, it can help individuals gain insight into how past experiences have affected their current thoughts and behaviors.

With continued therapy and support, adults who have experienced childhood trauma can find relief from debilitating symptoms and move towards a healthier sense of self.

Narrative exposure therapy (NET)

Narrative exposure therapy (NET) is a psychotherapeutic approach that has been seen to be effective in treating adult survivors of childhood trauma.

NET works by helping individuals to confront and process traumatic memories through the creation of a coherent narrative. This approach involves recounting past experiences in detail, including the sights, sounds, smells, and feelings associated with them.

Through this process, the individual gains insight into their experiences and begins to understand how they have shaped their beliefs about themselves and the world around them.

By confronting these memories in a safe and supportive environment, individuals are able to release emotional blockages that prevent healing from occurring.

Research has shown that NET can be particularly effective for those who have experienced multiple traumas or who struggle with complex PTSD.

This type of therapy may be used alone or as part of a broader treatment plan that includes other forms of therapy or medication management.

With patience, persistence, and the guidance of a skilled therapist, it is possible for adults to heal from childhood trauma using NET.

Prolonged exposure therapy (PE)

Prolonged exposure therapy (PE) is a type of cognitive-behavioral therapy that has proven to be effective in treating post-traumatic stress disorder (PTSD).

For adults who have experienced childhood trauma, PE can be a useful tool for healing. Through this therapy, individuals are encouraged to confront their traumatic experiences by recounting them out loud and revisiting the places and situations where they occurred. This approach helps individuals to gradually process their trauma by reducing their avoidance behavior.

PE works by exposing an individual to the feared stimulus repeatedly until he or she no longer responds with fear.

The therapist will first teach coping skills such as relaxation techniques, breathing exercises, and grounding methods before beginning the actual exposure exercise.

The patient may then be asked to describe or write about their traumatic event in detail while imagining it vividly in their mind.

While PE may sound daunting, research has shown that it can significantly reduce symptoms of PTSD, such as flashbacks, anxiety, depression, and sleep disturbances.

It is important for individuals undergoing PE treatment to work with a licensed therapist trained in this specific type of therapy who can provide support during the process.

With dedication and commitment, adults who have experienced childhood trauma have been able to find relief through prolonged exposure therapy.

Play therapy

Play therapy is a type of therapy that has been used for decades to help children overcome their emotional difficulties.

However, in recent years, it has been increasingly recognized as an effective treatment for adults who have suffered from childhood trauma.

Play therapy involves using various creative activities like art, music, and storytelling to help individuals express their feelings and emotions.

For adults who have experienced childhood trauma, play therapy provides a safe space where they can explore their past experiences and work through the complex emotions that come with them.

Through play therapy, adults can access parts of themselves that might be hard to reach through traditional talk therapies. It allows them to communicate symbolically and metaphorically in ways that are not always possible using words alone.

Overall, if you are an adult who has experienced childhood trauma and feels stuck or unable to move forward with your life, play therapy may be the right option for you.

 With its focus on creativity and self-expression, this approach can help you heal from past wounds while also providing a sense of empowerment and agency over your own story.

Art therapy

Art therapy is a powerful tool that can help adults heal from childhood trauma. It provides a safe and nurturing space where individuals can express their emotions, memories, and experiences through creative processes such as drawing, painting, or sculpting.

Creating art helps people access parts of themselves that may be hidden or difficult to verbalize. In addition, it allows them to explore and make sense of their thoughts and feelings in a non-threatening way.

Art therapy also provides an opportunity for individuals to reframe their traumatic experiences in a new light.

By creating artwork that represents their emotions or memories associated with the trauma, they are able to externalize those feelings rather than keeping them internalized. This process can help create distance between the individual and the traumatic experience, allowing them to gain perspective on what happened and begin the healing process.

Overall, art therapy offers a unique approach to healing from childhood trauma that combines creativity with therapeutic techniques.

Through this process of self-expression and growth, individuals can learn to manage their symptoms better while developing healthy coping mechanisms for dealing with future challenges.

Chapter Five
How to Recover from Rape and Sexual Trauma

Step 1: Open up about what happened to you

Opening up about sexual trauma and rape can be a difficult and emotional process, but it is essential in the journey towards recovery.

By sharing your experience with trusted friends, family members or healthcare professionals, you are taking the first step towards healing. It's necessary to note that there is no right or wrong way to open up about what happened to you - everyone's experiences are unique and personal.

When discussing your trauma, it's important to establish boundaries with those around you. Only share what feels comfortable for you, and don't feel pressured to disclose everything at once. If someone reacts negatively or dismissively, it's okay to distance yourself from them and seek support elsewhere. Remember that healing takes time, and there is no set timeline for when you should feel ready to share your story.

In addition, many survivors find strength in joining support groups or seeking therapy from professionals who specialize in treating sexual trauma survivors.

These individuals can provide guidance on coping mechanisms for dealing with triggers or flashbacks and help guide you through the healing process at a pace that works best for you.

Ultimately, opening up about what happened can be a transformative experience that helps survivors reclaim their power and move forward towards a brighter future.

Step2: Challenge your sense of helplessness and isolation

It is not unusual for survivors of rape and sexual trauma to feel helpless and isolated, especially in the aftermath of such a traumatic event.

However, it is important to challenge these feelings in order to begin the healing process. One way to do this is by seeking out support from loved ones or professional resources such as therapists or support groups.

Another important step in challenging helplessness and isolation is finding ways to regain a sense of control over one's life.

This could include setting boundaries with others, practicing self-care routines, or engaging in activities that bring a sense of empowerment or joy.

It may also involve confronting any negative thoughts or beliefs that have developed as a result of the trauma, such as feelings of shame or guilt.

Ultimately, recovering from rape and sexual trauma requires a commitment to self-care, self-compassion, and perseverance.

It may be a difficult journey at times, but with patience and determination, it is possible to overcome feelings of helplessness and isolation and reclaim one's sense of agency over their life.

Step3: Deal with feelings of guilt and shame

Dealing with guilt and shame after experiencing rape or sexual trauma can be a difficult journey.

Many survivors may feel like they are to blame for the assault, which can lead to intense feelings of guilt and self-blame. It's important to remember that the responsibility for the assault lies solely with the perpetrator, not with the survivor.

To start healing from these emotions, it's essential to acknowledge them first. Accepting that what happened was not your fault and allowing yourself to feel the pain associated with it is an important step toward recovery.

Talking about your feelings with a trusted friend or mental health professional can also help you process your emotions in a healthy way.

It's also crucial to work on building self-compassion and self-love. Always be mindful of the fact that you are deserving of love and respect, despite what happened in the past.

Practicing self-care activities such as meditation, exercise, or journaling can also help boost positive emotions while reducing negative ones like guilt and shame.

Remember that healing is a journey, but by taking steps towards self-love and acceptance, you can gradually move forward towards recovery from sexual trauma.

Below are some misconceptions that create the feeling of guilt and shame after rape and sexual abuse.

(a) **You didn't prevent the assault from happening:** Questioning what you did or didn't do after the act is simple. However, while you are under assault, your brain and body are in shock. You lack mental clarity.

A lot of folks claim to feel "frozen" during such moments. So, don't criticize yourself for having this normal response to trauma. You made the best of the difficult situation. You would have prevented the attack if you could have.

(b) **You trusted someone you "shouldn't" have:** The breach of trust is among the hardest things to handle after being assaulted by a person you know.

It's normal to begin second-guessing yourself and wondering if you missed any red flags. Just keep in mind that only the perpetrator is to blame. Don't punish yourself for thinking the perpetrator was a decent person.

The person who assaulted you should feel terrible and ashamed of himself and not you.

(c) **You were drunk or not cautious enough:** The only person accountable for the assault, regardless of the circumstances, is the perpetrator. You didn't deserve what happened to you or ask for it. Assign blame to the rapist, who should be held accountable.

Step4: Prepare for flashbacks and upsetting memories

Flashbacks and upsetting memories can be common experiences for survivors of rape and sexual trauma.

These intrusions can feel overwhelming and intense, leaving you feeling helpless and out of control. However, by preparing yourself ahead of time, you can minimize their impact on your life. One strategy is to create a safety plan, which involves identifying coping mechanisms that help ground you in the present moment when flashbacks arise.

This may include deep breathing exercises or engaging in sensory activities like holding onto an ice cube until it melts.

Another helpful approach is to develop a list of external resources that can provide support during difficult times.

This may include trusted friends or family members who know your situation and are available to talk if needed, as well as mental health professionals who specialize in treating trauma-related disorders such as PTSD (post-traumatic stress disorder).

Having these contacts readily accessible can help remind you that you are not alone and there are people who care about your well-being.

Lastly, practicing self-care habits like exercise, healthy eating, adequate sleep, and mindfulness meditation can also assist in managing symptoms related to flashbacks or intrusive thoughts.

By prioritizing these activities regularly, you will build resilience over time so that when challenging moments arise unexpectedly, it becomes easier to manage them with compassion and grace.

Remember that healing from sexual trauma takes time – be patient with yourself throughout the process!

Flashbacks and distressing memories can be reduced by doing the following:

> (a) **Try to anticipate triggers and be ready for them:** Anniversary dates, persons or locations connected to the rape, as well as specific sights, sounds, or odors, are examples of common triggers. Knowing what triggers may result in an emotional reaction may put you in a better position to comprehend what's happening and take action to calm down.
>
> (b) **Pay attention to any warning signs your body sends you:** When you start to feel anxious and frightened, your body and emotions offer you cues. Feeling tight, holding your breath, racing thoughts, shortness of breath, heat flushes, dizziness, and nausea are some of these signs.

(c) **Take action right away to comfort yourself:** It's crucial to take action promptly to calm yourself down when you experience any of the aforementioned symptoms to prevent a worsening of the situation. Slowing your breathing is one of the easiest and most efficient strategies to relieve anxiety and stress.

How to deal with flashbacks

You can't always stop flashbacks from arising. However, there are steps you may take if you start to feel out of the present and like the sexual attack is reoccurring.

Recognize the difference between flashback and reality

When experiencing a flashback, it's important to remind yourself that you are safe in the present moment.

It can be hard to differentiate between past trauma and current reality but try to focus on your surroundings and identify what is different from the traumatic event.

This will help ground you in the present and remind you that the flashback is not happening again.

Stay grounded in the present

WHEN FACED WITH FLASHBACKS, it is important to stay grounded in the present moment. This can be achieved through various grounding techniques such as deep breathing exercises, meditation, or mindfulness practices.

These techniques help individuals focus on their current surroundings and sensations rather than being overwhelmed by memories of past events.

Another effective way to stay grounded in the present is by engaging in physical activities that require concentration and attention to detail, such as yoga or martial arts.

These activities not only provide a sense of control but also serve as a healthy outlet for negative emotions.

It is important to remember that staying present does not mean suppressing or ignoring painful memories. Rather, it means acknowledging them while also recognizing that they are not happening in the current moment. By staying grounded and focusing on the present, individuals can gradually learn to manage their flashbacks and cope with trauma in a healthier way.

Step 5: Reconnect to your body and feelings

When recovering from rape or sexual trauma, it is important to reconnect with your body and feelings.

Trauma can often lead to a disconnection between the mind and the body, making it difficult to feel grounded and present in the moment. This disconnection can cause feelings of dissociation, numbness, or even physical pain.

One way to begin reconnecting with your body is through mindfulness practices such as meditation, breathing exercises or yoga. These practices can help ground you in the present moment by focusing on sensations within your body. It is also important to engage in physical activities that create positive experiences with your body, such as dancing or exercising.

Connecting with trusted friends and family members can also aid in this process by providing a safe space for you to express yourself and release pent-up emotions.

Step 6: Stay connected

Staying connected can be a crucial tool in the healing process for survivors of rape and sexual trauma.

It's not uncommon for survivors to feel isolated or disconnected from others after experiencing such a traumatic event.

However, connecting with others who have been through similar experiences can provide much-needed support and validation.

One way to stay connected is by joining a support group specifically for survivors of sexual assault. These groups offer a safe space where survivors can share their stories, receive emotional support, and learn coping mechanisms from one another.

Additionally, many organizations offer online forums or hotlines that are available 24/7 for survivors who may need someone to talk to.

Another way to stay connected is by participating in activities that bring joy and fulfillment.

This could include joining a sports team, taking up an art class, volunteering at a local organization, or simply spending time with friends and family members who provide love and encouragement.

Engaging in positive activities can help shift focus away from negative thoughts and emotions associated with the trauma while providing opportunities for new connections with like-minded individuals.

Step 7: Nurture yourself

One of the most crucial things to do when recovering from rape and sexual trauma is to nurture yourself. This means taking care of both your physical and emotional needs.

First, prioritize getting enough sleep, eating healthy foods, and engaging in regular exercise. These simple self-care practices can help support your overall well-being.

In addition to physical self-care, it's important to take time for emotional healing. Consider seeking professional therapy or counseling services to help work through any lingering trauma or negative emotions.

You may also find comfort in joining a support group with others who have experienced similar situations. Be gentle with yourself throughout the recovery process, and don't be afraid to seek out guidance or support when needed.

Finally, consider incorporating relaxation techniques into your daily routines, such as meditation, deep breathing exercises or yoga. These practices can help reduce stress levels which can be heightened after experiencing traumatic events like rape or sexual assault.

Remember that recovery is a journey, and it's important to take small steps each day towards healing and nurturing yourself back to physical and emotional health.

Step 8: See a therapist

Seeing a therapist can be a crucial step in recovering from rape and sexual trauma.

A trained professional can help survivors work through the emotional, psychological, and physical effects of these experiences. Therapists can provide a safe space for survivors to express their feelings, process traumatic memories, and develop coping strategies.

In therapy, survivors may explore issues such as guilt, shame, fear, anger, and self-blame.

They may also learn how to manage symptoms of post-traumatic stress disorder (PTSD), such as anxiety attacks or nightmares. Therapists may use a variety of approaches to support healing and growth, including cognitive-behavioral therapy (CBT), mindfulness practices, or art therapy.

It is important for survivors to find a therapist who specializes in treating trauma and who they feel comfortable working with.

Survivors may also choose between individual or group therapy sessions depending on their needs and preferences. Ultimately, seeing a therapist can be an empowering step towards reclaiming one's life after sexual violence.

Chapter Six
How to Build Your Self-Esteem After Experiencing Abuse

After going through abuse, rebuilding self-esteem can be a challenging and lengthy process. Individuals who have experienced abuse may struggle with feelings of worthlessness, shame, and guilt.

However, it's important to remember that healing is possible, and everyone deserves to feel confident in themselves.

Below are some steps you can take to rebuild your self-esteem and restore your confidence after your bad childhood experience.

Make a list of your own admirable qualities

One way to build self-esteem after going through abuse is to make a list of your admirable qualities. This list can help you focus on the positive aspects of yourself and counter any negative thoughts or beliefs that may have developed due to the abuse. It can be quite challenging to see your own strengths and accomplishments when you have experienced trauma, but taking the time to reflect on them can be empowering.

When making this list, it's important, to be honest with yourself and include even the smallest things that you are proud of. Maybe you are a good listener, or maybe you have a talent for cooking delicious meals.

These qualities may seem insignificant, but they all contribute to who you are as a person and should be celebrated.

Remember that building self-esteem takes time and effort, so don't feel discouraged if it doesn't come easily at first.

Keep adding to your list as you discover new things about yourself, and read over it whenever you need to remind yourself of your worth as an individual. Over time, this practice can help shift your mindset from one of victimhood to one of empowerment.

Quit trying to please everyone

One of the most effective steps you can take to build self-esteem after experiencing abuse is by quitting trying to please everyone.

For many people who have gone through traumatic experiences, it is a common tendency to seek validation and approval from others.

However, this constant need for external validation can lead to further emotional distress and low self-worth.

Instead of constantly seeking approval from others, you should focus on your own needs and desires.

By trusting yourself and making decisions based on what feels right for you, you can begin to develop a stronger sense of self-worth.

It is also important for you to recognize that you are not responsible for other people's happiness.

Trying to please everyone often means neglecting your own needs in favor of others. By prioritizing your own well-being, you can start feeling more confident in your abilities and worth as an individual.

Ultimately, building self-esteem after going through abuse requires a shift in mindset towards valuing oneself above pleasing others.

Build a positive self-image

Building a positive self-image can be a powerful tool in building self-esteem after going through abuse.

Recognizing and accepting oneself for who they are can help in overcoming the negative beliefs that may have been formed as a result of the abuse. By focusing on positive qualities and accomplishments, one can begin to see themselves in a more positive light.

The first step towards building a positive self-image is practicing self-care. Taking care of one's physical, emotional, and mental needs allows for an overall sense of well-being and confidence.

This includes things like healthy eating, exercise, meditation or mindfulness practices, therapy or counseling sessions, and engaging in activities that bring joy.

Set boundaries

Setting boundaries is a crucial step in building self-esteem after going through abuse. It involves identifying what behaviors and actions are unacceptable to you, communicating them clearly to others, and enforcing consequences when necessary.

By setting and maintaining healthy boundaries, survivors of abuse regain control over their lives and rebuild their sense of self-worth.

One way to set boundaries is to start small. This can involve saying no to invitations or requests that make you uncomfortable or speaking up when someone crosses a line with their behavior or language.

As you become more confident in your ability to assert yourself, you can gradually expand your boundaries and tackle more difficult situations.

It's important to remember that setting boundaries is not about punishing others or shutting them out of your life completely.

Rather, it's about creating a safe space for yourself where you can heal from past traumas and grow into the person you want to be. With time and practice, setting boundaries can become second nature and help survivors of abuse reclaim their power and confidence.

Believe you are deserving

It's a common feeling for individuals who have gone through abuse to feel as though they are unworthy or undeserving of love, success, or happiness.

The emotional and physical scars from the trauma can weigh heavily on self-esteem and create a destructive internal dialogue. However, it's important to remember that this negative self-talk is not rooted in truth.

Survivors of abuse are just as deserving of love and happiness as anyone else.

Building self-esteem after experiencing abuse is a journey that requires time and patience. It involves learning how to reframe negative thoughts into positive ones, practicing self-care, setting healthy boundaries, and seeking professional help if needed.

Creating achievable goals and celebrating small victories along the way can also help boost confidence.

It may be difficult to believe at first, but survivors of abuse possess immense strength and resilience.

By focusing on personal growth and healing, survivors can begin to see their worthiness shine through despite past experiences. With time, effort, and support from loved ones or professionals, building a positive sense of self-worth is possible for all survivors of abuse.

Take a stand for yourself

Standing up for yourself after going through abuse can be a crucial step toward building self-esteem.

When you assert your boundaries and demand respect, you are sending a powerful message to yourself and others that you value yourself enough to protect your well-being. This can help you feel more confident, empowered, and in control of your life.

Taking a stand also involves acknowledging that the abuse was not your fault and that you have the right to live free from harm. This shift in mindset can help counteract feelings of shame and guilt that often accompany abusive experiences, which can erode self-esteem over time.

It's important to remember that taking a stand doesn't necessarily mean confronting your abuser directly or engaging in conflict.

It can simply involve setting clear boundaries with others, seeking support from trusted friends or professionals, or practicing self-care activities like mindfulness or exercise.

Whatever form it takes, standing up for yourself is an act of courage and self-respect that can ultimately lead to greater confidence and well-being.

Stop comparing yourself to others

Comparing oneself to others can be a slippery slope, especially when it comes to building self-esteem after experiencing abuse. When we compare ourselves to those around us, we often find ourselves coming up short or feeling inadequate.

This can lead to further negative feelings about oneself and, consequently, lower self-esteem. By focusing on our personal growth and progress rather than comparing ourselves to others, we can begin to build a more positive sense of self-worth.

Furthermore, constant comparison with others is not only detrimental to our mental health but also hinders our ability to recognize and appreciate our unique qualities and strengths. It is vital that we learn how to celebrate our individuality instead of worrying about fitting into society's standards or the expectations of others.

In conclusion, stopping the habit of comparing oneself with others is crucial in rebuilding self-esteem after experiencing abuse.

It takes time and effort to cultivate a positive sense of self-worth, but by acknowledging your own journey and accomplishments as an individual, you will begin taking steps towards building a healthier relationship with yourself.

Celebrate your accomplishments

Acknowledging and recognizing your achievements can help you feel proud of yourself and give you a sense of accomplishment. It can also remind you that despite the challenges you have faced, there are things in your life that make you strong, capable, and worthy.

Celebrating small accomplishments along the way can also be helpful in building self-esteem. This could include completing a task at work or school, trying something new like cooking a meal from scratch or starting an exercise routine. Acknowledging these small wins helps shift the focus away from any negative thoughts or feelings that may arise from past abuse experiences.

Finally, celebrating accomplishments with others can also help build self-esteem. Sharing your success with friends or family who support and encourage you creates positive reinforcement for your achievements while strengthening relationships with those closest to you.

This boosts confidence and provides motivation to continue striving towards even more significant goals in the future.

Treat yourself with respect

When you've been through abuse, your sense of self-worth can be deeply damaged. You may struggle to believe that you deserve respect or kindness from others, let alone from yourself. However, treating yourself with respect is a powerful way to counteract these negative beliefs.

When you treat yourself with respect - by setting boundaries, practicing self-care, and being kind to yourself - you send a message to your mind and body that you are valuable and deserving of love and care.

This can help rebuild your sense of self-worth over time. Additionally, when you show respect towards yourself, it becomes easier to recognize when others are not treating you with the same level of consideration. This enables you to set boundaries in relationships that feel safe and respectful.

Furthermore, respecting oneself isn't just about sending signals outwardly but also about creating an inner dialogue that supports our growth as individuals in both personal and professional spheres.

Treating ourselves well is also essential for good mental health since it creates an environment where we can thrive emotionally and mentally by building resilience against stressors such as stigma or shame caused by past hurts or traumas we might have faced previously in our lives.

Have sessions of affirmations or positive self-talk

Rebuilding self-esteem can be a challenging and long process, especially if someone has gone through abuse.

However, incorporating sessions of affirmations or positive self-talk can be an essential tool in building self-esteem.

These techniques help people train their minds to focus on positive thoughts and emotions instead of negative ones.

Affirmations are simple statements that reflect what a person wants to achieve or how they want to feel about themselves. When repeated regularly, these phrases become ingrained in the subconscious mind and can positively impact one's mood and perspective. Positive self-talk involves focusing on one's strengths rather than weaknesses, encouraging oneself when facing challenges, and using kind words when talking to oneself.

Both techniques work by changing the inner dialogue from negative to positive thoughts, creating a more confident outlook on life.

As individuals begin to believe in themselves more through these exercises, their overall sense of self-worth increases.

In summary, practicing affirmations and positive self-talk helps individuals build confidence after going through abuse by changing how they think about themselves for the better.

Here are some examples of affirmations that can help:

1. "I am worthy and deserving of love and respect." This affirmation reminds survivors that they deserve to be treated with kindness and compassion.

2. "I am strong and capable." After going through a traumatic experience, it's easy to feel weak or powerless. This affirmation helps survivors recognize their inner strength.

3. "I trust myself to make the right decisions." Survivors may have had their autonomy taken away during the abuse, so this affirmation can help them regain confidence in their ability to make choices for themselves.

By incorporating these types of affirmations into daily life, survivors can begin to rebuild their sense of self-worth and overcome the negative messages they may have internalized as a result of the abuse they experienced.

It takes time and effort, but practicing positive self-talk is an important step towards healing from trauma.

Surround yourself with supportive people

Surrounding yourself with supportive people can play a crucial role in the process of building self-esteem, especially for those who have experienced abuse.

When someone goes through abuse, it is common for them to believe they are not worthy or deserving of kindness and support. Having a circle of understanding and supportive individuals can help counteract these negative beliefs.

Supportive people can provide emotional validation and encouragement that helps build a positive sense of self-worth.

They can offer practical assistance to manage daily tasks and responsibilities without judgment, which allows the individual time to focus on their healing journey.

Moreover, being surrounded by people who genuinely care about your well-being creates an environment free from criticism and negativity that may otherwise further damage one's already fragile self-esteem.

In conclusion, surrounding yourself with supportive individuals is essential when it comes to rebuilding self-esteem after experiencing abuse.

The support that these individuals offer is invaluable as they provide comfort, validation, practical assistance as well as foster an environment for growth and positivity.

Such a community reinforces the idea that you are deserving of love, respect and help you develop healthier coping mechanisms while combating negative beliefs caused by past experiences.

Conclusion

Healing from childhood trauma and hidden abuse is a complex and difficult journey that requires patience, self-compassion, and a willingness to confront the painful experiences of the past.

It is important to understand that healing is a process, and that there is no quick fix or one-size-fits-all approach.

However, with the right resources, support, and guidance, it is possible to overcome the effects of childhood trauma and hidden abuse and lead a fulfilling life.

One of the most important steps in healing from childhood trauma and hidden abuse is to acknowledge and validate the pain and suffering that was experienced.

This can be a challenging process, as many survivors of abuse may have been taught to minimize or ignore their feelings in order to survive. However, by allowing themselves to feel and express their emotions, survivors can begin to process the trauma and release it from their bodies and minds.

Another key aspect of healing is building a strong support system. This can include trusted friends and family members, mental health professionals, support groups, or other survivors of abuse.

Having a safe and supportive environment can help survivors to feel validated, heard, and understood, and can provide them with the strength and encouragement they need to continue their healing journey.

Therapy and other forms of professional support can also be invaluable tools in healing from childhood trauma and hidden abuse.

A skilled therapist can help survivors to identify and address the root causes of their trauma, develop coping strategies, and build skills for managing symptoms such as anxiety, depression, and post-traumatic stress disorder (PTSD).

Ultimately, healing from childhood trauma and hidden abuse requires a commitment to self-care and self-compassion.

This may involve taking time for rest and relaxation, engaging in activities that bring joy and fulfillment, and cultivating a positive and supportive relationship with oneself.

It is important to remember that healing is not a linear process, and that setbacks and challenges may arise along the way. However, with persistence and dedication, survivors of childhood trauma and hidden abuse can reclaim their lives and their sense of self-worth.

By embracing their own power and resilience, survivors can overcome the effects of abuse and create a life filled with joy, love, and connection.

Just Before You Go...

Now that you finished reading this book, what do you think of what you read?

Were there any tips or information you found insightful?

What do you think was missing from this book?

While you are reflecting on what you read, it would mean the world to me if you left an honest review.

As you know, reviews are integral to building relevancy for all content in online bookstores. So whether you found this information helpful or not, your candid review would help other customers and readers make an informed purchase.

Also, based on your reviews, I will either consolidate and keep up with my content quality or adjust this publication and future editions to create a better reading experience for my readers.

Do well to click the 'follow' icon on the author bio section, so you get notified whenever I upload a new book.

And finally, do well to check out my other related books:

- **Understanding and Parenting the Highly Sensitive Child**
- **Survival Guide for the Highly Sensitive Person**
- **Parent's Guide to Teen Depression**
- **Teens' Survival Guide for Depression and Anxiety**
- **How to Stop Being Negative**
- **Survival Guide for Racially Abused Persons**
- **Overcoming Self- Condemnation, and Low Self-Esteem**

Cheers...

Printed in Great Britain
by Amazon